# The Satanic Bible Magazine™

Creator, Founder, Editor, and Publisher
**George A. Hart**

**Volume 1, Issue 1.**
© George A. Hart 2015. No part of
The Satanic Bible Magazine may be
reproduced without prior written consent
from the publisher or copyright holders.

**ISBN**: 978-1-943287-00-0

**The Satanic Bible Magazine**
George A. Hart
ghpublish@gmail.com
732-552-6991

2

# Table of Contents

| | |
|---|---|
| Title Page | 1 |
| Table of Contents | 3 |
| Section 1: Articles & News | 4 |
|    1. Article and News Submissions | 5 |
|    2. High Priest Caesar 999 | 6 |
|    3. Spiritual Satanism 999 | 7 |
|    4. Church of The Antichrist 999 | 9 |
|    5. Temple of Satanic Kali | 11 |
|    6. The Holy Whore Priestess | 13 |
|    7. The Warrior-Priest | 15 |
| Section 2: Modeling & Photography | 16 |
|    1. Models and Photography Submissions | 17 |
| Section 3: Artwork & Poetry | 18 |
|    1. Artwork and Poetry Submissions | 19 |
| Section 4: Personals & Jobs | 20 |
|    1. Submissions & Information | 21 |
| Section 5: Advertising & Marketing | 22 |
|    1. Advertising and Marketing Submissions | 23 |
| Credits | 24 |

# Section 1: Articles & News

## Articles and News Submissions

Articles and News Submissions (Submitters will be paid these rates!) (Topics: Satanic, Vampire, Gothic, Metal Music, Tattoo, Nature, Hindu, Indian, Environment, Health, Sexual, Erotic, Tantra, Martial Arts, Ayurveda, etc.) ghpublish@gmail.com

1. Gothic Article $100 each
2. Vampire Article $100 each
3. Satanic Article $100 each
4. Nature Article $100 each
5. Hindu/Indian Article $100 each

# High Priest Caesar 999

I am an Author, Publisher, Mystic, Shaman, Tantric Healer, and Warrior-Priest. I often use my spiritual and pen name of Rev. Caesar 999, on many of my articles and books. I have been a practicing Satanic Mystic for over 20 years. Through my Spiritual Evolution, I have gone from being a Devil Worshiper, to an atheistic Laveyan Satanist, to a personal form of Theistic Satanism combined with aspects of Tantrism, Shakti Hinduism, Taoism, etc.

I focus upon Martial Arts, Spiritual Shamanic Development, Magickal Arts, Tantra and Tantric Healing, other healing arts, mystical communion with Self and Satanic Creation, worship of Satanic Creation in the form of the Goddess Kali (aka Satanic Kali), other deities, etc. I am the founder and High Priest of the underground Church of The Antichrist 999 and Temple of Satanic Kali. I am the creator of my own branch of Satanism, known as Spiritual Satanism 999.

I have written many Spiritual and Satanic books to help teach these beliefs and goals. I became my own publisher because it's difficult for new or unknown authors to break into the book market and also, so that I could help others like myself to publish their books as well.

I self-published my first book in 2005 ("Satan's Divine Vampir Bible" by Rev. Caesar 999), re-published in 2006 ("The Satanic Bible" by Rev. Caesar 999), and then again in 2007 ("The Satanic Bible" by Rev. Caesar 999) with the ISBN 978-0-615-16991-0. This is the foundational book for my mystical form of Spiritual Satanism which I call, Spiritual Satanism 999. I published a new updated version of this Satanic Bible in Nov. 2011, ("The Satanic Bible 2012" by Rev. Caesar 999). I also published, Satan's Sorcery Volume I, The Crystal Tower, The Quest, The Shadow Garden, and Welcome to Zone X.

I will be publishing many more books. If anyone wants to contact me to discuss my beliefs further or would like to publish your books through my services, then you are welcome to contact me.

Contact:
Rev. Caesar 999
drcaesar999@gmail.com

Published Books:
(The Satanic Bible - ISBN: 978-0-615-16991-0)
(The Satanic Bible 2012 - ISBN: 978-0-9840313-1-3, E-Book: 978-0-9840313-0-6)
(The Crystal Tower - ISBN 978-0-9840313-2-0, E-Book: 978-0-9840313-5-1)
(Satan's Sorcery Volume I - ISBN: 978-0-9840313-3-7, E-Book: 978-0-9840313-4-4)
(The Quest - ISBN: 978-0-9840313-6-8)
(The Shadow Garden - ISBN: 978-0-9840313-7-5)
(Welcome to Zone X - ISBN: 978-0-9840313-8-2)

# Spiritual Satanism 999

Spiritual Satanism 999 began its developmental journey many years ago in the mind of a Satanic Rebel. During that time, it was a teenager's disorganized and confused fantasy of a uniting concept, combining aspects of devil worship, heavy metal socializing, and dreams of popularity, friendships, beautiful women, and sexual fulfillment.

All of these dreams and fantasies, quickly burst into flames, as reality becomes a sobering enlightenment. The march toward organization and clarity began with knowledge, through research and many hours of book reading. Magickal Arts and Power became a method to achieve this goal. However, the goal itself began to change as I began to change and evolve.

I learned of atheism, selfishness, greed, and a mercenary lifestyle from Laveyan books and magickal and spiritual principles from Crowley books. During this time, I became more aware of my own rights and the rights of others in this world, along with all the suffering and Judeo-Christian based laws which strip away those rights, especially sexual rights. This revealed to me the core doctrines of the Judeo-Christian, which is truly their moral-value system.

Eventually, my belief structure began to develop into a combination of devil worship and atheistic Laveyan beliefs, with a focus upon fighting for and securing our rights. Meanwhile, the more I learned about magickal arts and the development of personal power, brought me to the conclusion that we all face limitations in this world. Some of us are far more limited than others and most of the people I had associated with, turned out to be nothing more than backstabbing pirates. This was what Lavey had in mind for an organization of Satanists? The lack of spirituality and the lack of education among most of the same type of people, make them nothing more than anti-spiritual pirates, which will achieve very little in the long run.

Spirituality and True Brotherhood and Sisterhood was the key to true unity and therefore a true religion must be born. From the ashes of magickal fantasies and power rituals, the New Phoenix was born and Satanism was reborn. Behold, the new religion of Satanism 999! This system combines the most spiritually unifying techniques with the most carnally fulfilling dreams! Everything that you desire spiritually and physically, can be found right here and now within this new age religion and I am its true messenger!

8

# Church of The Antichrist 999

The concept of a Church of The Antichrist first grew from my goal of organizing a religious society and community with the same beliefs and goals as myself. Also, the idea of a Church of The Antichrist was born out of a need to use superior organization to advance our goals and defeat our enemies. The major enemies of course being Judeo-Christian, which naturally defines my type of belief system as anti-Christian! Therefore, I ultimately represent anti-Christian beliefs and philosophy. These beliefs and goals naturally oppose many Judeo-Christian moral-values and moral views. These beliefs precede Christianity and Judaism, by many centuries!

I have to admit as well, the original close connection to the Christian concept of an Anti-Christ, which was an early motivation within my beliefs, but I have spiritually evolved beyond the basic Devil Worship beliefs and symbolism! However, it can still be an exhilarating, yet fantastic feeling to think of one's self as the embodiment of the Judeo-Christian archetype of pure evil in the minds of Christians, but at the same time consider myself a force for good for my people and myself! We always think of ourselves as being good and our enemies being evil or simply really bad people! Also, this plays upon their superstitions and our own. I certainly do not believe in Judeo-Christian superstitions and beliefs anymore!

This lets us naturally fall back upon our Adversarial Nature! Many of our moral-values and moral views precede Judeo-Christian values and beliefs. We naturally oppose Judeo-Christian beliefs and values and this makes us all Anti-Christs together! There is no single Anti-Christ and no superstitious biblical Anti-Christ! However, if our movement ultimately causes the collapse of Judeo-Christian civilization and they go into major decline, we can then possibly consider the title. Eventually, a powerful organization will bring the Judeo-Christian Empire to its knees and this organization will have a powerful leader. This powerful leader, can be seen as their superstitious Anti-Christ! However, in reality, this is just fantasy and fun fantasy!

Together, we will organize, develop, and strengthen an organization that will ultimately help our people secure our rights and spread our Spiritual Satanic culture to many worlds! We will spiritually evolve and keep our carnal lusts, maintaining a constant balance between our Spirituality and Carnal Nature! If you'd like to learn more about my beliefs, values, and goals, then you can read my many books, or email me directly.

# Temple of Satanic Kali

The Temple of Satanic Kali, is a re-imagining of my Church of The Antichrist 999. It's the more spiritual path for our people to naturally follow. We free our minds of thoughts of the Anti-Christ and begin to focus upon the Dark Mother Goddess Kali! She existed before all things and she is the foundation of everything! Praise Kali Ma! Praise Satanic Kali!

The ego must be surrendered and the self becomes one with Creation. Here we embrace our unity with the forces of Creation. We transcend the material and meditate deeply upon thoughts of true brotherhood and sisterhood, true love for our new family, and give ourselves over to this new family. Our desires are the desires of Kali and her consort of Shiva. We are all to be fulfilled and enlightened through this fulfillment!

The Holy Whore Priestess is resurrected and all of our pain and suffering, is softened and released through her Shakti Pleasures! She is the Great Shakti, the Great Shakta, the Great Dakini, and the Great Holy Whore Priestess! Through her Sexual Tantric Rituals, Dance, Yoga, and Deep Meditation, we are liberated from the tortures of un-fulfillment, liberated from unfulfilled desire, liberated from poverty slavery, liberated from starvation, liberated from joblessness, and liberated from homelessness! All of these things are what the Temple of Satanic Kali brings to the people!

12

# The Holy Whore Priestess

The Holy Whore Priestess and Priest, has existed in many regions, religions, and cultures around the world since ancient times! Today, very few of these religious traditions exist. Many of them involved Holy Whores, Prostitution, and Sexual Mysticism! We find the remnants of some of these religions and cultural traditions in India, Bangladesh, Tibet, China, etc. These religions and cultural traditions are connected to Shaktism, Kali Worship, Taoism, Buddhism, Tantrism, Yoga, Meditation, Classical Indian Dance Styles, and the Devadasi System, etc.

The modern Holy Whore Priestess and Priest, much like the ancients, fulfill the desires of those supporters in need and take on the aspects of the Goddess or God, Kali/Shiva, etc. The fulfillment of the desires of those who embody the Goddess Kali or God Shiva, reflects the foundational Tantric Creation story, where the copulation of the Goddess and God, brings about the manifestation of the material universe! Through this form of mystical union, we achieve a form of Spiritual Enlightenment and recognize our oneness with the Goddess/God.

Through Tantric Sexual Fulfillment, Dancing, Herbal Consumption, Wine, Meditation, Chanting, Music, and Ritualistic Ceremonies, we heal our bodies and minds! We become enlightened and spread the beauty of the Shakti Power and the worship of Shakti, Yellamma, Kali, other Goddesses, and Shiva!

If you'd like to join my order of Holy Whore Priests and Priestesses, then all you have to do is contact me and apply to join my temple! ghpublish@gmail.com

# The Warrior-Priest

The Warrior-Priest has existed since ancient times and in many cultures around the world! Today, I represent a new order of Warrior-Priests, based upon my religion of Spiritual Satanism 999. We combine aspects of meditation, spirituality, research, etc., with physical training that includes martial arts, yoga, tantra, etc. We practice these arts to improve the Physical Body and the Spiritual Body or the inner Spiritual Self!

Many know about the Warrior-Priests of India or the Buddhist Shaolin Monks, etc. These Warrior-Priests reached great achievements. Over centuries these Monks became famous for their skills and defense of the people. The job of our Warrior-Priests is also to defend our people and our temple!

It's better to begin your training at a younger age, but any age is good to start, because there will always be benefits to your health, body and spirit! It's important to develop a spiritual health consciousness and become aware of our surroundings. We do not force a fanatical or strict moral code upon our Warrior-Priests, but we do hold our Satanic Moral-Code. The Satanic Moral-Code, teaches us to be respectful to our people and supporters. This is one of the more important values!

When we train the body and mind, we develop a sense of humbleness and a controlled ego. This does not mean that we will have absolutely no ego, just one that knows its place in the world. We do not want our people to be completely super egotistic, which will blind them and others to their own weaknesses and faults! We are a community, as well as a true brotherhood and sisterhood. We are not a selfish mercenary group!

Our Warrior-Priests can be male or female. Usually, during the first initiation ritual, the Warrior-Priest has their head shaven! This head shaving is symbolic of initiation and sacrifice! We should continue to renew our initiation throughout our lives by shaving our heads again and again. However, this is only necessary if you feel the need or if you have gone astray from your path. Also, during winter months, it may not be practical to enforce this rule.

If you would like to join my order of Warrior-Priests, then all you must do is to contact me and apply to join my Church or Temple! ghpublish@gmail.com

# Section 2: Modeling & Photography

# *Models and Photography Submissions*

Models (Topics: Satanic, Vampire, Gothic, Metal Music, Tattoo, Nature, Hindu, Indian, Environment, Health, Sexual, Erotic, Tantra, Martial Arts, Ayurveda, etc.) Models can contact me directly, to arrange a photoshoot! ghpublish@gmail.com

1. $100 non-nude photoshoot
2. $500 semi-nude photoshoot (Adult Magazines Only)
3. $1000 full-nude photoshoot (Adult Magazines Only)

Photos Submissions (Submitters will be paid these rates!)(Topics: Satanic, Vampire, Gothic, Metal Music, Tattoo, Nature, Hindu, Indian, Environment, Health, Sexual, Erotic, Tantra, Martial Arts, Ayurveda, etc.) ghpublish@gmail.com

1. Gothic $50 each
2. Vampire $50 each
3. Satanic $50 each
4. Nature $50 each
5. Hindu/Indian $50 each

## Section 3: Artwork & Poetry

# *Artwork and Poems Submission*

Artwork Submissions (Submitters will be paid these rates!)(Topics: Satanic, Vampire, Gothic, Metal Music, Tattoo, Nature, Hindu, Indian, Environment, Health, Sexual, Erotic, Tantra, Martial Arts, Ayurveda, etc.) ghpublish@gmail.com

1. Gothic $50 each
2. Vampire $50 each
3. Satanic $50 each
4. Nature $50 each
5. Hindu/Indian $50 each

Poems Submissions (Submitters will be paid these rates!)(Topics: Satanic, Vampire, Gothic, Metal Music, Tattoo, Nature, Hindu, Indian, Environment, Health, Sexual, Erotic, Tantra, Martial Arts, Ayurveda, etc.) ghpublish@gmail.com

1. Gothic $50 each
2. Vampire $50 each
3. Satanic $50 each
4. Nature $50 each
5. Hindu/Indian $50 each

# Section 4: Personals & Jobs

## *Personals and Job Submissions*

Personals and Job Submissions (Less than 50 Words!) ghpublish@gmail.com

1. 1 Personal Listing with 2 photos $25
2. 1 Job Listing $25

# Section 5: Advertising & Marketing

## *Advertising and Marketing Submissions*

Advertising and Marketing Submissions (Submitters will be paid these rates!)(Topics: Satanic, Vampire, Gothic, Metal Music, Tattoo, Nature, Hindu, Indian, Environment, Health, Sexual, Erotic, Tantra, Martial Arts, Ayurveda, etc.) ghpublish@gmail.com

1. Full page $100 per year. (When monthly $100 per month)
2. Half page $50 per year. (When monthly $50 per month)
3. Business card size $25 per year. (When monthly $25 per month)

## Credits

All Articles by Rev. Caesar 999
All Image Artwork is Public Domain, Found on
Wikipedia.com or MaaDurgaWallpaper.com
Layout and Design by George A. Hart

*TheSatanicBibleMagazine.com*

*ghpublish@gmail.com*